The Growth Mindset Blueprint

Transforming Challenges into Triumphs'

Gerard Assey

The Growth Mindset Blueprint
Transforming Challenges into Triumphs'
By
Gerard Assey
© Copyright 2023 by Author

Published by:
Gerard Assey
19/18, Palli Arasan Street
Anna Nagar East
Chennai - 600 102

ISBN: 978-93-92492-89-1

(Image courtesy Freepik: 'https://www.freepik.com' Thank You)

Table of Contents

Preface
Introduction
What is a Growth Mindset?
The Power of Mindset: Fixed vs. Growth
Benefits of Developing a Growth Mindset

Part I: Understanding Mindsets
The Foundation of Mindsets: Beliefs and Attitudes
Fixed Mindset: The Limiting Beliefs
Growth Mindset: The Path to Success

Part II: Cultivating a Growth Mindset
Embracing Challenges: Stepping Stones to Growth
Embracing Failure: A Learning Opportunity
Persistence and Resilience: Nurturing Growth
The Role of Effort and Practice in Development
Seeking Feedback: Constructive Criticism for Growth
The Power of Positive Self-Talk

Part III: Applying a Growth Mindset
Goal Setting and Planning for Growth
Overcoming Procrastination and Self-Doubt
Developing Adaptability and Flexibility
Fostering Creativity and Innovation
Building Strong Relationships and Networks
Leading with a Growth Mindset

Part IV: Nurturing a Growth Mindset in Different Areas
Nurturing a Growth Mindset in Education and Lifelong Learning

Nurturing a Growth Mindset in Career Development and Advancement
Nurturing a Growth Mindset in Personal Relationships and Communication
Nurturing a Growth Mindset in Health and Wellness
Nurturing a Growth Mindset in Emotional Intelligence and Self-Awareness

Part V: Challenges and Roadblocks
Common Obstacles to Developing a Growth Mindset
Overcoming Imposter Syndrome
Dealing with Setbacks and Plateaus

Part VI: Action Plan, Exercises & Activities
Self-Assessment: Where Do You Stand on the Mindset Spectrum?
Step-by-Step Master Action Plan: Developing a Growth Mindset
Exercises and Activities for Developing a Growth Mindset
31 Growth Mindset Affirmations: 1 Each Day of the Month

Part VII: The Journey into Developing a Growth Mindset
The Journey Ahead: Continuing Your Growth Mindset Development
Inspiring Success Stories of Growth Mindset Champions
Final Thoughts and Reflections

Conclusion
About the Author

Preface

Welcome to the journey of transformation and personal growth that awaits you within the pages of this book. In a world that is constantly evolving, where challenges and opportunities abound, the concept of a growth mindset has emerged as a beacon of empowerment and change. This book is your guide to embracing this powerful mindset, unlocking your full potential, and achieving a life filled with continuous learning, resilience, and success.

At its core, **'The Growth Mindset Blueprint-** *Transforming Challenges into Triumphs'* is not just a book; it's a roadmap for a mindset revolution. In these pages, we delve deep into the psychology of mindset, exploring the distinctions between fixed and growth mindsets and revealing the transformative impact that cultivating a growth mindset can have on every facet of your life.

This journey begins by understanding the fundamental beliefs and attitudes that shape your mindset. We explore the limitations of a fixed mindset and the boundless possibilities that a growth mindset offers. Through real-life examples, actionable strategies, and thought-provoking exercises, you'll embark on a step-by-step process of self-discovery and personal development.

As you progress through each chapter, you'll learn how to:

- ✓ Embrace challenges as stepping stones to growth and excellence.
- ✓ Reframe failures as valuable lessons and opportunities for improvement.

- ✓ Develop persistence, resilience, and a willingness to embrace effort.
- ✓ Seek feedback, constructive criticism, and use it to elevate your skills.
- ✓ Harness the power of positive self-talk to overcome obstacles.
- ✓ Foster adaptability, creativity, and innovation in all aspects of life.
- ✓ Set and achieve meaningful goals through the lens of growth.
- ✓ Cultivate a growth mindset in education, career, relationships, health, and more.
- ✓ Overcome common obstacles and navigate setbacks with unwavering resilience.

This book is not a mere collection of theories; it's a practical toolkit designed to empower you to take actionable steps toward embracing a growth mindset. Whether you're a student striving for academic excellence, a professional navigating a competitive career landscape, or an individual seeking personal fulfillment, the principles outlined in these pages are universally applicable.

As you journey through the chapters, I encourage you to engage fully with the exercises, reflect on the examples, and apply the strategies in your daily life. Remember that developing a growth mindset is a continuous process, a journey of self-discovery, and a commitment to personal evolution. It's about recognizing your potential, embracing challenges with open arms, and forging a path to success that is uniquely yours.

I invite you to embark on this enlightening expedition toward a growth-oriented life. Let the wisdom and insights within this book guide you as you uncover the boundless potential that resides within you. May you walk away from these pages equipped with the tools, knowledge, and inspiration to thrive, overcome obstacles, and become the architect of your own growth story.

Here's to unleashing your inner potential and mastering the art of a growth mindset.

Introduction

- ✓ What is a Growth Mindset?
- ✓ The Power of Mindset: Fixed vs. Growth
- ✓ Benefits of Developing a Growth Mindset

Introduction

In a world where challenges are abundant and opportunities ever-evolving, your mindset serves as the compass that guides your journey. The concept of a growth mindset has gained significant attention in recent years for its profound impact on personal and professional development. At its core, a growth mindset is a transformative belief system that shapes how you perceive your abilities, approach challenges, and ultimately, the trajectory of your success.

What is a Growth Mindset?
A growth mindset is an attitude that embraces the belief in the malleability of one's abilities and intelligence. Individuals with a growth mindset perceive challenges and setbacks as opportunities for learning and growth, rather than as indications of their limitations. This mindset fosters a sense of curiosity, resilience, and a willingness to embrace discomfort in order to reach new heights.
Example: Imagine two students faced with a challenging math problem. The student with a growth mindset would view this challenge as a chance to expand their mathematical skills and put in the effort to solve the problem. In contrast, a student with a fixed mindset might become frustrated, seeing the problem as evidence of their lack of inherent mathematical talent.

The Power of Mindset: Fixed vs. Growth
Understanding the distinction between a fixed mindset and a growth mindset is pivotal to unlocking

your potential. A fixed mindset is characterized by the belief that your abilities and intelligence are static traits, set in stone from birth. This mindset often leads to avoiding challenges, fearing failure, and feeling threatened by the success of others.

Conversely, a growth mindset operates on the premise that abilities can be developed through dedication, effort, and learning. This mindset empowers you to embrace challenges, persist in the face of setbacks, and view failures as stepping stones to success.

Example: Consider two entrepreneurs presented with a business setback. The entrepreneur with a fixed mindset might view the setback as a sign that they're not cut out for business and may give up. On the other hand, the entrepreneur with a growth mindset would approach the setback as an opportunity to learn, adapt their strategies, and come back stronger.

Benefits of Developing a Growth Mindset

Cultivating a growth mindset has a ripple effect across all areas of your life, bringing forth a multitude of benefits that extend beyond personal development:

- ✓ **Resilience**: A growth mindset equips you with the mental resilience to navigate challenges and setbacks with a positive attitude. Instead of being deterred by failures, you're motivated to persist and improve.
- ✓ **Learning and Skill Development**: With a growth mindset, you're more inclined to embrace new knowledge and skills. You recognize that continuous learning is essential for personal and professional growth.

- ✓ **Increased Effort and Persistence**: Individuals with a growth mindset are willing to put in the effort needed to achieve their goals. Challenges are seen as opportunities to enhance their abilities, driving them to work harder.
- ✓ **Innovation and Creativity**: Embracing a growth mindset encourages innovative thinking. You're more likely to explore new ideas and experiment with different approaches, leading to creative solutions.
- ✓ **Positive Relationships**: A growth mindset fosters empathy and understanding in relationships. You're open to feedback, appreciate the success of others, and collaborate effectively.

Action Plan: Cultivating a Growth Mindset

1. **Self-Reflection**: Take time to reflect on your current beliefs about abilities and challenges. Identify areas where a fixed mindset might be holding you back.
2. **Embrace Challenges**: Choose a small challenge outside your comfort zone. Approach it with the intention to learn and grow, even if success isn't immediate.
3. **Change Your Internal Dialogue**: Pay attention to your self-talk. When faced with a setback, reframe your thoughts from "I can't do this" to "I haven't mastered this yet."
4. **Learn from Failure**: Recall a past failure and analyze what you learned from it. How can you apply these lessons moving forward?
5. **Seek Feedback**: Request constructive feedback from a colleague or friend on a

specific skill. Use their insights to improve and grow.

6. **Set Growth Goals**: Choose a skill or area you want to develop. Set specific, measurable goals and create a plan to achieve them.

7. **Celebrate Effort and Progress**: Acknowledge your efforts and progress along the way, regardless of the outcome. This reinforces the value of the growth process.

In this journey of developing a growth mindset, you're embarking on a transformative path that has the potential to revolutionize the way you approach challenges and achieve success. By embracing the principles of a growth mindset, you're primed to unlock your fullest potential and embrace a future filled with continuous growth and achievement.

Part I: Understanding Mindsets

- ✓ The Foundation of Mindsets: Beliefs and Attitudes
- ✓ Fixed Mindset: The Limiting Beliefs
- ✓ Growth Mindset: The Path to Success

Part I: Understanding Mindsets

The Foundation of Mindsets: Beliefs and Attitudes

Your beliefs and attitudes form the bedrock of your mindset, influencing how you perceive yourself and the world. These deeply ingrained perspectives shape your reactions to challenges, failures, and successes. By delving into the foundation of mindsets, you can lay the groundwork for understanding and developing a growth mindset.

At its core, a mindset is a collection of beliefs about your abilities, talents, and potential. These beliefs color your attitude toward opportunities and setbacks, determining whether you approach them with openness or trepidation.

Examples:

- ✓ **Fixed Belief:** A person believes that their artistic talent is innate and cannot be improved. They avoid taking art classes or trying new artistic techniques.
- ✓ **Growth Belief:** Another person believes that with dedication and practice, they can improve their artistic skills over time. They eagerly enroll in art classes and experiment with new techniques.

Action Plans and Strategies:

- ✓ **Self-Discovery:** Reflect on your current beliefs about your abilities and talents. Identify areas where you may be holding fixed beliefs.
- ✓ **Challenge Your Assumptions:** Take one area where you believe your abilities are fixed.

Engage in deliberate practice and measure your progress over time.
- ✓ **Cultivate a Growth Attitude:** Approach challenges with curiosity and a willingness to learn. View setbacks as opportunities for improvement rather than signs of incapability.
- ✓ **Affirmation and Visualization:** Develop affirmations that counter fixed beliefs and visualize your potential for growth. Repeat these affirmations regularly.

Fixed Mindset: The Limiting Beliefs

A fixed mindset is akin to a self-imposed prison of limiting beliefs. When you have a fixed mindset, you view your abilities as static and unchangeable. This perspective can hold you back, making you fearful of challenges and causing you to give up prematurely. People with a fixed mindset often:

- ✓ **Avoid Challenges:** They fear exposing their perceived lack of ability and prefer to stick to what they already know.
- ✓ **Shy Away from Effort:** They believe that if they need to exert effort, it's a sign of their inherent shortcomings.
- ✓ **Fear Failure:** They view failure as a reflection of their inadequacy rather than an opportunity for growth.
- ✓ **Feel Threatened by Others' Success:** The achievements of others can trigger insecurity and self-doubt.

Examples:

- ✓ **Fear of Failure:** An individual declines a leadership role at work because they worry that they might not excel in it.

✓ **Avoiding Challenges:** A student avoids joining a debate club because they fear they may not be naturally gifted at public speaking.

Action Plans and Strategies:
✓ **Identify Fixed Mindset Patterns:** Become aware of situations or thoughts that trigger your fixed mindset. Note down instances where you shy away from challenges or downplay your abilities.
✓ **Reframe Setbacks:** When you encounter a setback, focus on the lessons you can learn from it rather than viewing it as a validation of your limitations.
✓ **Celebrate Effort and Progress:** Reward yourself for putting in effort, regardless of the outcome. Recognize that growth happens through perseverance and hard work.
✓ **Embrace Challenges:** Purposefully seek out challenges that stretch your abilities. Embrace them as opportunities for growth.

Growth Mindset: The Path to Success
A growth mindset is a transformative belief system that fuels your journey toward success. With a growth mindset, you understand that your abilities and intelligence can be developed through effort, learning, and resilience. This perspective empowers you to face challenges head-on and embrace failures as stepping stones to achievement.

Individuals with a growth mindset tend to:
✓ **View Challenges as Opportunities:** They approach challenges with enthusiasm, recognizing that they provide a chance to learn and improve.

- ✓ **Persist Through Setbacks:** They embrace failure as a natural part of the learning process and are resilient in the face of obstacles.
- ✓ **Embrace Effort and Practice:** They understand that mastery is a result of dedicated effort and continuous practice.
- ✓ **Seek Feedback and Critique:** They actively seek feedback from others to enhance their skills and knowledge.
- ✓ **Inspire Others:** They uplift and encourage those around them, valuing collaboration and mentorship.

Examples:

- ✓ **Learning from Failure:** A scientist conducts an experiment that doesn't yield the expected results. Instead of giving up, they analyze the outcome to refine their hypothesis and approach.
- ✓ **Seeking Feedback:** An entrepreneur presents a business idea to a mentor and actively seeks feedback to improve their concept.

Action Plans and Strategies:

- ✓ **Practice Positive Self-Talk:** Replace self-doubt with affirmations that emphasize your potential for growth and improvement.
- ✓ **Set Growth Goals:** Define clear goals that reflect your desire to learn and develop. Break these goals into actionable steps.
- ✓ **Learn from Failure:** When faced with failure, ask yourself what you can learn from the experience. How can you use this feedback to enhance your skills and strategies?
- ✓ **Cultivate a Learning Mindset:** Approach challenges with an attitude of curiosity and a

desire to learn. Focus on the journey rather than solely on the destination.

✓ **Seek Feedback:** Actively seek feedback from mentors, peers, or experts in your field. Use their insights to refine your skills and strategies.

By understanding the foundation of mindsets, recognizing the constraints of a fixed mindset, and embracing the empowering perspective of a growth mindset, you embark on a transformative journey toward success and self-discovery. The path to a growth mindset is within your reach, and as you adopt this mindset, you open doors to uncharted possibilities and pave the way for a future filled with continuous growth and achievement.

Part II: Cultivating a Growth Mindset

- ✓ Embracing Challenges: Stepping Stones to Growth
- ✓ Embracing Failure: A Learning Opportunity
- ✓ Persistence and Resilience: Nurturing Growth
- ✓ The Role of Effort and Practice in Development
- ✓ Seeking Feedback: Constructive Criticism for Growth
- ✓ The Power of Positive Self-Talk

Part II: Cultivating a Growth Mindset

Embracing Challenges: Stepping Stones to Growth

Challenges are not obstacles to avoid but rather opportunities for growth and self-discovery. Embracing challenges with a growth mindset propels you forward on your journey of personal and professional development.

Examples:

- ✓ **Professional Challenge:** An employee takes on a project that requires learning new skills. Despite initial difficulties, they remain determined and eventually master the skills needed to succeed.
- ✓ **Personal Challenge:** A fitness enthusiast sets a goal to run a marathon, even though they've never run long distances before. They face physical and mental challenges during training but persevere and successfully complete the marathon.

Action Plans and Strategies:

- ✓ **Choose Growth-Oriented Challenges:** Seek out challenges that align with your personal and professional goals. Choose tasks that push you out of your comfort zone.
- ✓ **Shift Your Perspective:** Instead of viewing challenges as threats, reframe them as opportunities for growth and learning.
- ✓ **Break Down Challenges:** Divide larger challenges into smaller, manageable steps. Focus on mastering each step before moving on to the next.

✓ **Celebrate Effort:** Acknowledge and celebrate your efforts and progress, regardless of the immediate outcome.

Embracing Failure: A Learning Opportunity

Failure is not a destination; it's a stepping stone on the path to success. A growth mindset allows you to view failure as a valuable learning opportunity rather than a reflection of your worth.

Examples:

✓ **Professional Failure:** A startup founder's first business venture fails, but they use the experience to identify mistakes, learn valuable lessons, and eventually launch a successful second venture.

✓ **Academic Failure:** A student receives a low grade on a test, prompting them to seek additional help and study strategies to improve their performance.

Action Plans and Strategies:

✓ **Reframe Failure:** Instead of dwelling on failure, focus on the lessons and insights you can gain from the experience.

✓ **Analyze Mistakes:** Reflect on what went wrong and why. Identify specific actions you can take to avoid making the same mistakes in the future.

✓ **Seek Support:** Reach out to mentors, colleagues, or friends for guidance and advice when facing failure.

✓ **Embrace Growth from Failure:** Share your failure stories and the lessons you've learned with others. This helps normalize the concept of failure as a part of the growth process.

Persistence and Resilience: Nurturing Growth
Persistence and resilience are the cornerstones of a growth mindset. These qualities enable you to overcome setbacks, stay focused on your goals, and continue striving for improvement.
Examples:
- ✓ **Career Persistence:** An aspiring writer receives numerous rejection letters but continues submitting their work until they finally secure a publishing deal.
- ✓ **Academic Resilience:** A student faces challenges in a difficult course but seeks help from tutors, adjusts their study approach, and ultimately earns a passing grade.

Action Plans and Strategies:
- ✓ **Set Resilience Goals:** Develop strategies to cope with setbacks, such as setting aside time to reflect on challenges and strategize solutions.
- ✓ **Cultivate Perseverance:** When faced with obstacles, remind yourself of your long-term goals and the value of persistence.
- ✓ **Mindfulness and Self-Care:** Practice techniques such as mindfulness meditation, exercise, and maintaining a healthy work-life balance to enhance your resilience.
- ✓ **Learn from Adversity:** Reflect on past challenges and setbacks. What did you learn from those experiences, and how can you apply those lessons moving forward?

The Role of Effort and Practice in Development
Effort and practice are the engines that drive growth and mastery. A growth mindset recognizes that

consistent effort and deliberate practice are essential for achieving excellence.

Examples:
- ✓ **Music Mastery:** A musician dedicates hours of daily practice to improve their instrument-playing skills, gradually achieving mastery over time.
- ✓ **Language Learning:** An individual commits to consistent language practice, gradually improving their fluency and communication skills.

Action Plans and Strategies:
- ✓ **Set SMART Goals:** Define Specific, Measurable, Achievable, Relevant, and Time-bound goals for skill improvement.
- ✓ **Create a Routine:** Establish a consistent practice routine to develop skills and knowledge over time.
- ✓ **Deliberate Practice:** Focus on specific areas that need improvement, breaking down complex tasks into manageable components.
- ✓ **Seek Feedback:** Regularly solicit feedback from mentors, peers, or experts to refine your practice techniques and identify areas for growth.

Seeking Feedback: Constructive Criticism for Growth

Feedback is a valuable tool for growth and improvement. Embracing feedback with an open and growth-oriented mindset allows you to identify areas for development and refine your skills.

Examples:
- ✓ **Professional Feedback:** An employee actively seeks feedback from their supervisor

on their performance, leading to targeted development opportunities.
  - ✓ **Creative Critique:** An artist shares their work with peers, welcoming constructive criticism to refine their artistic techniques.

Action Plans and Strategies:
  - ✓ **Create a Feedback Network:** Establish relationships with mentors, colleagues, and peers who can provide constructive feedback.
  - ✓ **Ask for Specific Feedback:** When seeking feedback, ask for specific insights on areas you're looking to improve.
  - ✓ **Active Listening:** When receiving feedback, practice active listening and avoid becoming defensive. Focus on understanding and learning from the feedback.
  - ✓ **Implement Feedback:** Use feedback to make tangible improvements and adjustments to your skills and strategies.

The Power of Positive Self-Talk

Your inner dialogue shapes your beliefs and actions. Positive self-talk, rooted in a growth mindset, empowers you to overcome self-doubt, build confidence, and navigate challenges.

Examples:
  - ✓ **Before a Presentation:** A professional tells themselves, "I've prepared thoroughly, and I have the skills to deliver a successful presentation."
  - ✓ **Facing a Challenge:** An athlete reminds themselves, "I may not have mastered this yet, but with effort and practice, I can improve."

Action Plans and Strategies:
- ✓ **Self-Awareness:** Pay attention to your inner dialogue and recognize when negative thoughts arise.
- ✓ **Challenge Negative Thoughts:** When you catch yourself thinking negatively, challenge those thoughts with evidence of your past successes and growth.
- ✓ **Practice Affirmations:** Develop positive affirmations that counter self-doubt and reinforce your potential for growth.
- ✓ **Visualize Success:** Visualize yourself succeeding in challenging situations, reinforcing your belief in your abilities.

By cultivating the habits of embracing challenges, viewing failure as an opportunity, nurturing persistence and resilience, recognizing the value of effort and practice, seeking feedback, and harnessing the power of positive self-talk, you lay the groundwork for a transformative growth mindset. These strategies empower you to navigate obstacles, embrace opportunities, and continue your journey toward personal and professional development.

Part III: Applying a Growth Mindset

- ✓ Goal Setting and Planning for Growth
- ✓ Overcoming Procrastination and Self-Doubt
- ✓ Developing Adaptability and Flexibility
- ✓ Fostering Creativity and Innovation
- ✓ Building Strong Relationships and Networks
- ✓ Leading with a Growth Mindset

Part III: Applying a Growth Mindset

Goal Setting and Planning for Growth
Goal setting is a vital tool for harnessing the power of a growth mindset. By setting clear, achievable goals and creating a strategic plan, you create a roadmap for your personal and professional development.
Examples:
- ✓ **Career Goals:** An employee sets a goal to enhance their leadership skills by attending workshops, seeking mentorship, and taking on leadership roles within their organization.
- ✓ **Learning Goals:** A student sets a goal to improve their time management skills by creating a study schedule and seeking guidance from academic advisors.

Action Plans and Strategies:
- ✓ **Define SMART Goals:** Set Specific, Measurable, Achievable, Relevant, and Time-bound goals that align with your growth aspirations.
- ✓ **Break Down Goals:** Divide larger goals into smaller, manageable steps to track progress and maintain motivation.
- ✓ **Create a Plan:** Develop a detailed plan outlining the actions, resources, and timeline required to achieve your goals.
- ✓ **Review and Adjust:** Regularly review your goals and make adjustments based on your progress and changing circumstances.

Overcoming Procrastination and Self-Doubt
Procrastination and self-doubt can hinder your growth journey. Embracing a growth mindset helps

you overcome these obstacles and take confident steps toward your goals.

Examples:
- ✓ **Procrastination:** An individual sets aside time each day to work on a challenging project, gradually building momentum and overcoming procrastination.
- ✓ **Self-Doubt:** A writer acknowledges their self-doubt but continues writing, reminding themselves that improvement comes with practice and effort.

Action Plans and Strategies:
- ✓ **Set Small Tasks:** Break tasks into small, manageable steps to overcome the overwhelm that often leads to procrastination.
- ✓ **Focus on Progress:** Shift your attention from perfection to progress. Embrace the idea that imperfect action is better than no action.
- ✓ **Challenge Negative Thoughts:** When self-doubt arises, counter it with evidence of your past achievements and growth.
- ✓ **Reward Yourself:** Celebrate small wins along the way to boost your confidence and motivation.

Developing Adaptability and Flexibility

In a rapidly changing world, adaptability and flexibility are essential traits. A growth mindset empowers you to embrace change, learn new skills, and thrive in dynamic environments.

Examples:
- ✓ **Career Adaptability:** An employee eagerly takes on new responsibilities and adapts their skills to the evolving needs of their organization.

- ✓ **Personal Adaptability:** An individual learns a new technology tool to improve their productivity, despite initial challenges.

Action Plans and Strategies:
- ✓ **Continuous Learning:** Commit to lifelong learning to stay relevant and adaptable in your field.
- ✓ **Embrace Change:** Approach changes with curiosity and a willingness to learn. Focus on the opportunities that change can bring.
- ✓ **Experiment and Learn:** Try new approaches, techniques, or methods to enhance your skills and knowledge.
- ✓ **Seek Diverse Experiences:** Step out of your comfort zone by engaging in activities outside of your usual routine.

Fostering Creativity and Innovation

A growth mindset nurtures your capacity for creativity and innovation. By embracing experimentation and open-mindedness, you can unlock your creative potential and drive innovation.

Examples:
- ✓ **Creative Problem-Solving:** A team member proposes unconventional solutions to a project challenge, sparking innovative discussions within the group.
- ✓ **Personal Creativity:** An individual explores various hobbies and artistic pursuits, allowing their creativity to flourish.

Action Plans and Strategies:
- ✓ **Encourage Curiosity:** Explore new topics, industries, or disciplines to expand your knowledge and perspective.

- ✓ **Brainstorm Freely:** Engage in brainstorming sessions where no idea is off-limits. Embrace the process of generating creative solutions.
- ✓ **Experiment with Ideas:** Implement and test new ideas, even if they carry an element of risk. Learning from failures contributes to innovation.
- ✓ **Collaborate:** Engage in collaborative projects and discussions to gather diverse insights and generate innovative solutions.

Building Strong Relationships and Networks

A growth mindset extends to your interactions with others. Cultivating meaningful relationships and networks enriches your personal and professional growth.

Examples:
- ✓ **Networking:** A professional attends industry conferences and networking events to connect with peers and learn from their experiences.
- ✓ **Mentorship:** An individual seeks mentorship from an experienced professional to gain insights and guidance in their career.

Action Plans and Strategies:
- ✓ **Actively Listen:** Practice active listening to understand others' perspectives and experiences.
- ✓ **Connect Authentically:** Build genuine relationships based on mutual respect and shared interests.
- ✓ **Seek Mentorship:** Identify mentors who can provide guidance, share insights, and support your growth journey.

✓ **Collaborate:** Engage in collaborative projects and initiatives to expand your network and learn from others.

Leading with a Growth Mindset

Leaders who embody a growth mindset inspire and empower those around them. By leading with a growth-oriented approach, you foster a culture of continuous learning and development.

Examples:

✓ **Leadership Communication:** A manager encourages their team to share ideas, engage in open dialogue, and learn from failures.

✓ **Innovation Promotion:** An organizational leader promotes a culture where employees are encouraged to experiment, take calculated risks, and learn from setbacks.

Action Plans and Strategies:

✓ **Model Growth:** Demonstrate a willingness to learn, adapt, and seek feedback as a leader.

✓ **Foster Learning Opportunities:** Provide resources, workshops, and training programs that promote ongoing skill development.

✓ **Acknowledge Effort and Improvement:** Recognize and reward employees who demonstrate a growth mindset and exhibit a commitment to learning.

✓ **Encourage Risk-Taking:** Create an environment where employees feel comfortable taking calculated risks and experimenting with new ideas.

As you apply the principles of a growth mindset to set goals, overcome procrastination and self-doubt, develop adaptability and flexibility, foster creativity, build relationships, and lead with a growth-oriented approach, you are creating a life rich with opportunities for development and success. By embracing growth-oriented strategies, you navigate challenges with confidence, continually refine your skills, and inspire those around you to embrace their own journey of growth and achievement.

Part IV: Nurturing a Growth Mindset in Different Areas

- ✓ Nurturing a Growth Mindset in Education and Lifelong Learning
- ✓ Nurturing a Growth Mindset in Career Development and Advancement
- ✓ Nurturing a Growth Mindset in Personal Relationships and Communication
- ✓ Nurturing a Growth Mindset in Health and Wellness
- ✓ Nurturing a Growth Mindset in Emotional Intelligence and Self-Awareness

Part IV: Nurturing a Growth Mindset in Different Areas

Nurturing a Growth Mindset in Education and Lifelong Learning

A growth mindset is a powerful asset in education and lifelong learning, enabling you to embrace challenges, learn from failures, and continuously expand your knowledge and skills.

Examples:

- ✓ **Education:** A student faces a challenging subject but approaches it with curiosity, seeking additional resources and study techniques to improve their understanding.
- ✓ **Lifelong Learning:** An individual commits to learning a new language, dedicating time each day to practice and immersing themselves in the language.

Action Plans and Strategies:

- ✓ **Set Learning Goals:** Define specific learning objectives and break them down into achievable milestones.
- ✓ **Adopt a Curious Mindset:** Approach new subjects and topics with a sense of curiosity and a desire to explore.
- ✓ **Embrace Continuous Learning:** Seek out opportunities for professional development, workshops, courses, and online resources to enhance your skills.
- ✓ **Reflect and Apply:** After learning new concepts, reflect on how you can apply them in real-world situations to reinforce your understanding.

Nurturing a Growth Mindset in Career Development and Advancement

A growth mindset propels your career development, enabling you to overcome challenges, adapt to changing circumstances, and pursue continuous improvement.

Examples:

- ✓ **Career Transition:** An individual shifts to a new role in a different industry, embracing the challenge as an opportunity to learn and grow.
- ✓ **Professional Development:** A professional seeks out mentorship and additional training to enhance their leadership skills and advance in their career.

Action Plans and Strategies:

- ✓ **Set Career Goals:** Define clear, achievable career goals that align with your aspirations and values.
- ✓ **Seek Skill Enhancement:** Identify skills relevant to your desired career path and actively work to develop and improve them.
- ✓ **Network and Connect:** Engage in networking events, conferences, and workshops to expand your professional circle and learn from others.
- ✓ **Embrace Challenges:** Volunteer for challenging projects and responsibilities to gain experience and showcase your growth-oriented mindset.

Nurturing a Growth Mindset in Personal Relationships and Communication

A growth mindset enhances your interpersonal interactions, allowing you to navigate conflicts, improve communication, and foster positive connections with others.

Examples:
- ✓ **Conflict Resolution:** A person engages in open and empathetic communication during a disagreement, seeking to understand the other person's perspective.
- ✓ **Effective Communication:** An individual actively works on their communication skills, seeking feedback and adjusting their approach based on the responses of others.

Action Plans and Strategies:
- ✓ **Practice Active Listening:** Focus on truly understanding others by listening without judgment and asking clarifying questions.
- ✓ **Seek Feedback:** Ask for feedback on your communication style and be open to making adjustments based on the input you receive.
- ✓ **Embrace Empathy:** Put yourself in others' shoes to better understand their feelings, perspectives, and experiences.
- ✓ **Healthy Conflict Resolution:** Approach conflicts with a growth-oriented mindset, seeking to find common ground and solutions that benefit all parties.

Nurturing a Growth Mindset in Health and Wellness

A growth mindset extends to your approach to health and wellness, empowering you to set and achieve goals, overcome setbacks, and prioritize self-care.

Examples:
- ✓ **Fitness Goals:** An individual sets fitness goals and approaches challenges, such as weight loss or muscle gain, with a growth

mindset, continuously adjusting their exercise routine and nutrition.
- ✓ **Mental Well-being:** A person practices mindfulness and meditation, acknowledging that developing emotional resilience takes time and consistent effort.

Action Plans and Strategies:
- ✓ **Set Health Goals:** Define specific health and wellness objectives that align with your overall well-being.
- ✓ **Adopt a Balanced Approach:** Embrace a balanced lifestyle that includes regular exercise, healthy eating, rest, and relaxation.
- ✓ **Overcome Setbacks:** When facing challenges or setbacks, focus on the progress you've made and seek support from health professionals or therapists.
- ✓ **Practice Self-Compassion:** Treat yourself with kindness and understanding, recognizing that well-being is a journey that requires patience and effort.

Nurturing a Growth Mindset in Emotional Intelligence and Self-Awareness

A growth mindset enhances your emotional intelligence and self-awareness, enabling you to regulate your emotions, manage stress, and navigate complex situations.

Examples:
- ✓ **Stress Management:** An individual practices mindfulness techniques to manage stress and develop emotional resilience.
- ✓ **Self-Awareness:** A person engages in self-reflection to identify their emotional triggers

and patterns, seeking opportunities for personal growth.

Action Plans and Strategies:
- ✓ **Practice Mindfulness:** Engage in mindfulness exercises to increase awareness of your emotions and thought patterns.
- ✓ **Journaling:** Maintain a journal to reflect on your emotions, reactions, and experiences, allowing for deeper self-awareness.
- ✓ **Develop Empathy:** Practice understanding others' emotions and perspectives to enhance your emotional intelligence and strengthen relationships.
- ✓ **Embrace Growth from Challenges:** When faced with emotional challenges, view them as opportunities for personal development and growth.

In each of these areas-education, career, relationships, health, and emotional intelligence-nurturing a growth mindset enriches your experiences, enables you to overcome obstacles, and empowers you to continuously evolve and achieve success. By applying growth-oriented strategies to these aspects of your life, you unlock your potential and create a fulfilling and purposeful journey of growth and self-discovery.

Part V: Challenges and Roadblocks

- ✓ Common Obstacles to Developing a Growth Mindset
- ✓ Overcoming Imposter Syndrome
- ✓ Dealing with Setbacks and Plateaus

Part V: Challenges and Roadblocks

Common Obstacles to Developing a Growth Mindset

While the journey toward a growth mindset is transformative, it's not without its challenges. Recognizing and overcoming common obstacles is essential to nurturing and sustaining this mindset.

Examples:
- ✓ **Self-Doubt:** A person questions their ability to learn new skills and grow, leading to hesitation in pursuing new opportunities.
- ✓ **Fear of Failure:** An individual avoids challenges due to a deep-seated fear of failing and the perceived impact on their self-worth.

Action Plans and Strategies:
- ✓ **Self-Reflection:** Regularly reflect on your beliefs and attitudes. Identify moments when fixed mindset thoughts arise.
- ✓ **Mindset Awareness:** When faced with challenges, consciously shift your perspective from fixed to growth by reminding yourself of your potential for learning and improvement.
- ✓ **Seek Support:** Engage with mentors, coaches, or therapists who can help you navigate mindset challenges and provide guidance.
- ✓ **Positive Affirmations:** Develop affirmations that counter negative thoughts and reinforce your commitment to growth. Repeat them regularly.

Overcoming Imposter Syndrome

Imposter syndrome is the feeling of inadequacy and the fear of being exposed as a fraud despite evidence of your competence. Overcoming imposter syndrome is a critical step in cultivating a growth mindset.

Examples:

- ✓ **Success Acknowledgment:** An individual takes time to acknowledge their achievements and attributes their successes to their efforts and abilities.
- ✓ **Seeking Feedback:** A professional actively seeks feedback to gain perspective on their skills and areas for improvement, reducing self-doubt.

Action Plans and Strategies:

- ✓ **Track Achievements:** Maintain a record of your accomplishments, both big and small, to remind yourself of your capabilities.
- ✓ **Normalize Mistakes:** Understand that making mistakes is a natural part of learning and growth. Embrace them as opportunities for improvement.
- ✓ **Visualize Success:** Visualize yourself confidently succeeding in situations that trigger imposter syndrome.
- ✓ **Share Experiences:** Open up about your feelings of imposter syndrome with trusted friends or mentors who can provide support and perspective.

Dealing with Setbacks and Plateaus

Setbacks and plateaus are inevitable on the path to growth. Learning how to navigate these moments with a growth mindset is essential for sustained progress.

Examples:
- ✓ **Setback Resilience:** A person experiences a professional setback but views it as a chance to learn and adjust their approach.
- ✓ **Plateau Response:** An individual recognizes a plateau in their skill development and seeks new challenges to reignite their growth.

Action Plans and Strategies:
- ✓ **Reframe Setbacks:** View setbacks as opportunities to learn, adjust, and improve rather than as permanent failures.
- ✓ **Analyze and Adjust:** When facing a setback, analyze what went wrong, identify lessons, and adjust your strategies accordingly.
- ✓ **Seek Learning Opportunities:** During plateaus, actively seek out new challenges or learning experiences to reignite your growth journey.
- ✓ **Practice Patience:** Understand that growth is not always linear; plateaus are part of the process. Be patient and trust the process.

By understanding and addressing these common obstacles, overcoming imposter syndrome, and navigating setbacks and plateaus with a growth mindset, you equip yourself with the tools to persevere and thrive on your journey of personal and professional development. Embrace challenges as opportunities, transform self-doubt into self-empowerment, and learn from setbacks to continue your path of growth and achievement.

Part VI: Action Plan, Exercises & Activities

- ✓ Self-Assessment: Where Do You Stand on the Mindset Spectrum?
- ✓ Step-by-Step Master Action Plan: Developing a Growth Mindset
- ✓ Exercises and Activities for Developing a Growth Mindset
- ✓ 31 Growth Mindset Affirmations: 1 Each Day of the Month

Part VI: Action Plan, Exercises & Activities

Self-Assessment: Where Do You Stand on the Mindset Spectrum?

This comprehensive self-assessment is to gauge where you currently stand on the mindset spectrum – from a fixed mindset to a growth mindset. This exercise will help you identify your existing beliefs and attitudes, laying the foundation for your growth mindset journey.

Step 1: Reflect on Your Beliefs

Take a moment to reflect on your beliefs about abilities, learning, challenges, and failure. Consider the following statements and indicate whether you agree or disagree with each one. Be honest with yourself and trust your initial response.

- ✓ People are born with a certain level of intelligence, and there's not much they can do to change it.
  - ☐ Agree ☐ Disagree
- ✓ I often avoid challenges because I'm worried about failing or looking incompetent.
  - ☐ Agree ☐ Disagree
- ✓ Effort is more important than talent or intelligence when it comes to achieving success.
  - ☐ Agree ☐ Disagree
- ✓ Feedback and criticism are valuable opportunities for growth and improvement.
  - ☐ Agree ☐ Disagree

✓ When I encounter setbacks, I tend to give up rather than persisting and trying again.
☐ Agree ☐ Disagree
✓ I believe that my abilities and skills can be developed with dedication, practice, and learning.
☐ Agree ☐ Disagree

Step 2: Reflect on Your Past Experiences

Think about specific situations from your past where you faced challenges, setbacks, or failures. Reflect on how you responded and what thoughts and emotions were prevalent during those times. Consider the following questions:

✓ How did you react when you encountered a significant challenge or setback in the past?
☐ I tended to avoid the challenge or give up quickly.
☐ I approached the challenge with determination and a willingness to learn.
✓ How do you typically view your past failures or mistakes?
☐ I view them as evidence of my limitations or lack of ability.
☐ I view them as opportunities for learning and growth.
✓ How do you handle receiving feedback or criticism from others?
☐ I often feel defensive and resistant to feedback.
☐ I appreciate feedback as a chance to improve and make adjustments.

Step 3: Reflect on Your Goals and Aspirations

Consider your current goals and aspirations – both short-term and long-term. Reflect on how your mindset influences your approach to these goals.

- ✓ When pursuing a new goal or skill, how do you typically respond to initial challenges or difficulties?
  - ☐ I tend to feel discouraged and question my ability.
  - ☐ I see challenges as natural and part of the learning process.
- ✓ How do you view setbacks or slow progress in relation to your goals?
  - ☐ I interpret setbacks as signs that I may not have what it takes.
  - ☐ I see setbacks as temporary obstacles that can be overcome with effort and perseverance.
- ✓ How open are you to seeking new experiences and learning opportunities, even if they are outside of your comfort zone?
  - ☐ I prefer to stick to what I know and avoid unfamiliar situations.
  - ☐ I actively seek out new experiences to expand my knowledge and skills.

Step 4: Interpret Your Results

Based on your responses, calculate your score for each mindset category- fixed mindset and growth mindset.

Assign 1 point for each "Agree" response in the fixed mindset category (statements 1, 2, and 5) and 1 point for each "Disagree" response in the growth mindset category (statements 3, 4, and 6).

Fixed Mindset Score: _____ out of 3

Growth Mindset Score: _____ out of 3

Interpretation:

- ✓ If your fixed mindset score is higher, you may tend to lean towards a fixed mindset in certain areas of your life.

✓ If your growth mindset score is higher, you may already embrace a growth mindset or have a predisposition toward it.

Step 5: Reflection and Action

Reflect on your self-assessment results and consider the following questions:

✓ What insights have you gained about your current mindset based on your self-assessment?

✓ In which areas of your life do you notice a more fixed mindset approach, and in which areas do you tend to exhibit a growth mindset?

✓ What specific actions can you take to further develop and nurture a growth mindset in those areas where you want to see improvement?

Remember, this self-assessment is a starting point on your journey to cultivating a growth mindset. Use your insights to set intentions and take actionable steps toward embracing a growth-oriented perspective in all aspects of your life. As you continue your growth mindset development, periodically revisit this self-assessment to track your progress and celebrate your achievements.

Step-by-Step Master Action Plan: Developing a Growth Mindset

1. Self-Awareness: Recognize Your Current Mindset
   - ✓ Example: Identify moments when you shy away from challenges or doubt your abilities. Reflect on times when you've attributed success or failure solely to fixed traits.
   - ✓ Action: Keep a journal to record instances of fixed mindset thinking and behaviors.
2. Education: Learn About Growth Mindset
   - ✓ Example: Read books, articles, or watch videos about growth mindset. Understand the key principles and benefits of embracing a growth mindset.
   - ✓ Action: Set aside 30 minutes each day to study growth mindset literature and resources.
3. Mindset Shifting: Reframe Challenges and Failures
   - ✓ Example: Instead of avoiding a difficult project, view it as an opportunity to enhance your skills and learn something new.
   - ✓ Action: When facing a challenge, consciously remind yourself that it's a chance for growth and learning.
4. Embrace Effort: Celebrate Hard Work
   - ✓ Example: Acknowledge the effort you put into a presentation, even if the outcome wasn't perfect.
   - ✓ Action: Whenever you accomplish a task, reflect on the effort you invested and give yourself credit for it.

5. **Seek Feedback: Embrace Constructive Criticism**
   - ✓ Example: After a presentation, ask colleagues for feedback on areas for improvement rather than solely focusing on positive comments.
   - ✓ Action: Approach a mentor or colleague for feedback on a recent project and take notes on their suggestions.
6. **Continuous Learning: Set Learning Goals**
   - ✓ Example: Decide to learn a new skill, such as coding, and set incremental goals to track your progress.
   - ✓ Action: Create a list of skills you want to develop and set achievable goals for each.
7. **Overcome Setbacks: Reframe Failures as Lessons**
   - ✓ Example: If a project doesn't yield the expected results, reflect on what you've learned from the experience and how you can apply it next time.
   - ✓ Action: When faced with a setback, analyze what went wrong and focus on the lessons learned.
8. **Positive Self-Talk: Challenge Negative Thoughts**
   - ✓ Example: Replace "I can't do this" with "I haven't mastered this yet, but I'm making progress."
   - ✓ Action: Practice catching and reframing negative thoughts with growth-oriented alternatives.
9. **Visualization: Envision Success**
   - ✓ Example: Before a job interview, visualize yourself confidently answering questions and impressing the interviewer.

✓ Action: Set aside time each morning to visualize successful outcomes for upcoming tasks or challenges.

10. Mentorship: Seek Guidance and Support

✓ Example: Approach a colleague you admire and ask for advice on developing a growth mindset.

✓ Action: Identify potential mentors or role models and initiate a conversation about your growth journey.

11. Mindfulness: Focus on the Present

✓ Example: When facing a difficult task, concentrate on the immediate steps you need to take, rather than getting overwhelmed by the whole process.

✓ Action: Practice mindfulness exercises to stay present and grounded in your daily activities.

12. Celebrate Progress: Recognize Your Achievements

✓ Example: After completing a difficult project, treat yourself to a small reward to acknowledge your effort and growth.

✓ Action: Create a ritual to celebrate your accomplishments, no matter how big or small.

13. Networking: Connect with Growth-Minded Individuals

✓ Example: Attend a workshop or seminar where you can meet people who share your enthusiasm for personal development.

✓ Action: Join online communities or attend events that bring together individuals interested in growth mindset.

14. Reflect and Adjust: Regular Self-Check

- ✓ Example: At the end of each week, review your progress, celebrate achievements, and identify areas for improvement.
- ✓ Action: Set aside time for a weekly reflection session to track your growth mindset journey.
15. Consistency: Make Growth Mindset a Habit
- ✓ Example: Integrate growth mindset practices into your daily routine, such as journaling, positive self-talk, and seeking challenges.
- ✓ Action: Set reminders and establish routines to ensure you consistently engage in growth mindset activities.

Remember, developing a growth mindset is an ongoing process. Consistently practicing these steps and strategies will gradually shift your perspective, helping you embrace challenges, learn from setbacks, and continuously evolve towards your full potential.

31 Ways to Develop and Nurture a Growth Mindset

Here are 31 ways, one for each day of the month that you can use to develop and nurture a growth mindset:

1. **Embrace Challenges:** Seek out new challenges, both big and small, as opportunities for growth.
2. **View Effort as a Path to Mastery:** Understand that effort is a necessary part of learning and improving.
3. **Cultivate Curiosity:** Ask questions and explore new topics to expand your knowledge.
4. **Persist in the Face of Setbacks:** When you encounter obstacles, persist and keep moving forward.
5. **Replace "Not Yet" for "Failure":** Instead of saying "I failed," say "I haven't mastered it yet."
6. **Value the Process Over the End Result:** Focus on the journey and the learning process, not just the outcome.
7. **Learn from Mistakes:** Analyze your mistakes to discover valuable lessons and opportunities for growth.
8. **Seek Constructive Feedback:** Welcome feedback as a tool for improvement, not as criticism.
9. **Inspire Others:** Share your growth mindset journey and inspire those around you.
10. **Set Goals:** Establish specific, achievable goals that challenge you to grow.

11. **Visualize Success:** Visualize yourself achieving your goals and believe in your ability to do so.
12. **Practice Mindfulness:** Stay present in the moment and be open to new experiences.
13. **Celebrate Effort:** Celebrate your hard work and dedication, regardless of the outcome.
14. **Use Positive Self-Talk:** Replace negative thoughts with positive, growth-oriented affirmations.
15. **Read and Learn:** Read books and articles on topics that interest you and expand your knowledge.
16. **Mentor Others:** Share your expertise and help others on their own growth journeys.
17. **Learn from Role Models:** Study the lives and achievements of individuals you admire.
18. **Step Out of Your Comfort Zone:** Challenge yourself to try new things and take risks.
19. **Network and Connect:** Build relationships with like-minded individuals who support your growth.
20. **Reflect on Your Progress:** Regularly assess your growth and set new goals for improvement.
21. **Adapt to Change:** Embrace change as an opportunity for learning and personal development.
22. **Teach Others:** Teaching reinforces your own understanding and helps others grow.
23. **Overcome Self-Doubt:** Recognize and challenge your self-limiting beliefs.
24. **Stay Persistent:** Keep going even when the path to success is difficult or unclear.

25. **Learn from Criticism:** Use criticism as a chance to gain insight and improve.
26. **Accept Responsibility:** Take ownership of your actions and their consequences.
27. **Practice Gratitude:** Appreciate the progress you've made and the opportunities you have.
28. **Keep a Journal:** Document your growth mindset journey, including challenges and successes.
29. **Stay Open to Feedback:** Seek out different perspectives and be open to changing your views.
30. **Collaborate with Others:** Work with others to solve problems and learn from their expertise.
31. **Never Stop Learning:** Understand that growth is a lifelong journey; there's always more to discover.

Incorporate these daily practices into your life, and over time, you'll find that your growth mindset becomes an integral part of your approach to challenges and opportunities.

Exercises and Activities for Developing a Growth Mindset

Here is a collection of engaging and effective exercises and activities designed to help you actively develop and nurture a growth mindset. Each exercise is designed to challenge your beliefs, promote self-awareness, and encourage positive change.

Exercise 1: Embracing Challenges

Challenge yourself to step out of your comfort zone by taking on a new activity or skill you've never tried before. It could be learning a musical instrument, cooking a new recipe, or attempting a DIY project. Reflect on the experience and the lessons you learned.

Exercise 2: Reframing Failure

Identify a recent setback or failure you've experienced. Write down three positive aspects or lessons that emerged from the situation. Consider how these insights contribute to your growth and development.

Exercise 3: Growth Mindset Journaling

Keep a journal dedicated to your growth mindset journey. Each day, write down at least one challenge you faced, how you approached it with a growth mindset, and the positive outcomes you observed.

Exercise 4: Feedback Reflection

Seek out constructive feedback from a colleague, friend, or mentor. When receiving feedback, focus on listening without defensiveness and ask clarifying questions to understand their perspective. Take notes on their insights and your plan for improvement.

Exercise 5: Visualization for Success
Set aside time for visualization. Close your eyes and vividly imagine yourself successfully achieving a specific goal. Engage your senses and emotions, visualizing every detail. Embrace the feelings of accomplishment and use this visualization to motivate your actions.

Exercise 6: Self-Compassion Practice
Practice self-compassion by writing a letter to yourself as if you were offering support to a dear friend. Acknowledge any challenges or setbacks you're experiencing and offer words of encouragement and understanding.

Exercise 7: Growth Mindset Affirmations
Create a list of personalized growth mindset affirmations that resonate with you. Repeat these affirmations daily, both in the morning and before bed, to reinforce your growth-oriented beliefs.

Exercise 8: Reflecting on Progress
At the end of each week, take time to reflect on your growth mindset journey. Write a brief summary of your achievements, challenges you overcame, and insights you gained. Celebrate your progress and identify areas for continued growth.

Exercise 9: Goal Setting with a Growth Mindset
Identify a specific goal you want to achieve. Break it down into smaller, manageable steps and create a timeline for completion. Embrace setbacks as learning opportunities and adjust your plan as needed.

Exercise 10: Growth Mindset Peer Discussion
Engage in a growth mindset discussion with a peer or friend. Share your experiences, challenges, and successes related to developing a growth mindset.

Listen to their insights and exchange strategies for further growth.

Exercise 11: Mindful Observation

Select an object in your surroundings and spend a few minutes observing it closely. Note its details, textures, and colors. Reflect on how this practice of mindful observation enhances your ability to focus and learn.

Exercise 12: Gratitude and Growth

Keep a gratitude journal where you write down three things you're grateful for each day. As you express gratitude, also reflect on how each experience contributes to your personal growth and well-being.

Exercise 13: Overcoming Limiting Beliefs

Identify a limiting belief you hold about yourself or your abilities. Write down evidence that challenges this belief, showcasing times when you demonstrated skills, resilience, or growth in similar situations.

Exercise 14: Learning from Role Models

Identify a role model or someone you admire for their growth mindset. Research their journey, challenges, and successes. Write a brief reflection on the lessons you can apply to your own growth mindset development.

Exercise 15: Positive Self-Talk Practice

Consciously monitor your inner dialogue throughout the day. Whenever you catch yourself engaging in negative self-talk or doubt, reframe the thought with a positive and growth-oriented perspective.

Remember, consistency is key. Engage in these exercises regularly, adapting them to your unique preferences and needs. Over time, you'll cultivate a strong and resilient growth mindset that empowers you to navigate challenges, embrace opportunities, and achieve your full potential.

31 Growth Mindset Affirmations: 1 Each Day of the Month

Here are 31 growth mindset affirmations, one for each day of the month that you can use to cultivate a positive and growth-oriented mindset. Feel free to use these affirmations as daily reminders to reinforce your growth mindset and inspire positive change in your life. Repeat them regularly, internalize their messages, and watch as your mindset transforms over the course of the month.

Day 1: *"I embrace challenges as opportunities for growth and learning."*
Day 2: *"My efforts and persistence will lead me to success."*
Day 3: *"I am capable of adapting and thriving in any situation."*
Day 4: *"I am resilient in the face of setbacks and failures."*
Day 5: *"I choose to see failures as stepping stones to my success."*
Day 6: *"I am open to new experiences and eager to learn."*
Day 7: *"Every day, I am becoming a better version of myself."*
Day 8: *"I believe in my ability to overcome challenges with determination."*
Day 9: *"I am in control of my thoughts, and I choose positivity."*
Day 10: *"I am constantly improving and progressing toward my goals."*
Day 11: *"I have the power to turn obstacles into opportunities."*

Day 12: *"I am capable of learning and mastering new skills."*

Day 13: *"I am worthy of success and all the good things that come my way."*

Day 14: *"I embrace feedback as a valuable tool for growth."*

Day 15: *"I am confident in my ability to handle challenges with grace."*

Day 16: *"I trust in my capacity to overcome any challenges that come my way."*

Day 17: *"I am resilient, and setbacks only make me stronger."*

Day 18: *"I am committed to my personal and professional growth."*

Day 19: *"I have the courage to step outside my comfort zone and embrace new opportunities."*

Day 20: *"I am the creator of my own success story."*

Day 21: *"I am open to trying new things and learning from every experience."*

Day 22: *"I am patient with myself and trust the process of growth."*

Day 23: *"I am capable of achieving greatness through dedication and hard work."*

Day 24: *"I am resilient in the face of challenges and setbacks."*

Day 25: *"I am constantly expanding my skills and knowledge."*

Day 26: *"I believe in my potential to achieve my dreams."*

Day 27: *"I am focused and determined to reach my goals."*

Day 28: *"I am the architect of my own growth and success."*

Day 29: *"I am worthy of success, and I embrace opportunities to shine."*

Day 30: *"I choose positivity, even in the face of adversity."*
Day 31: *"I am on a continuous journey of growth and self-improvement."*

Part VII: The Journey into Developing a Growth Mindset

- ✓ The Journey Ahead: Continuing Your Growth Mindset Development
- ✓ Inspiring Success Stories of Growth Mindset Champions
- ✓ Final Thoughts and Reflections

Part VII: The Journey into Developing a Growth Mindset

As you reach the conclusion of this journey into developing a growth mindset, take a moment to reflect on the profound transformation you've undergone. You've explored the foundations of mindsets, learned strategies to cultivate and apply a growth mindset in various areas of your life, and tackled common obstacles that can hinder your progress. As you embark on the journey ahead, remember that developing a growth mindset is an ongoing process that requires dedication, self-awareness, and continuous effort.

Action Plans and Strategies:

- ✓ **Reflect on Your Progress:** Take time to reflect on how far you've come in embracing a growth mindset. Acknowledge the changes you've made and the challenges you've overcome.
- ✓ **Celebrate Achievements:** Celebrate your achievements and successes, both big and small, as a testament to your commitment to growth.
- ✓ **Set New Goals:** Identify new areas of your life where you can apply and further develop your growth mindset. Set specific goals and create action plans to achieve them.

The Journey Ahead: Continuing Your Growth Mindset Development

Your journey toward a growth mindset doesn't end here. It's a lifelong endeavor that requires ongoing dedication. As you move forward, commit to nurturing your growth mindset and integrating it into all aspects of your life.

Examples:
- ✓ **Ongoing Learning:** Continuously seek out new opportunities for learning and skill development, whether through formal education, workshops, or self-directed study.
- ✓ **Challenging Comfort Zones:** Regularly challenge yourself to step outside of your comfort zones and embrace new challenges.

Action Plans and Strategies:
- ✓ **Learning Agenda:** Create a personal learning agenda that outlines the skills, knowledge, and experiences you want to pursue in the coming months and years.
- ✓ **Regular Reflection:** Set aside time for regular self-reflection to assess your progress, identify areas for improvement, and adjust your strategies as needed.
- ✓ **Accountability Partner:** Consider partnering with a friend, colleague, or mentor who can support and hold you accountable for your growth mindset goals.

Inspiring Success Stories of Growth Mindset Champions

Throughout history, many individuals have demonstrated the power of a growth mindset in achieving remarkable success. These stories serve as a testament to the transformative potential of embracing a growth-oriented perspective.

Examples:
- ✓ **Thomas Edison:** Despite numerous failures, Edison persisted in his pursuit of inventing the

light bulb, demonstrating the value of resilience and learning from setbacks.
- ✓ **J.K. Rowling:** Rowling's persistence in the face of rejection and adversity led to the creation of the immensely successful "Harry Potter" series.

Action Plans and Strategies:
- ✓ **Study Success Stories:** Research and study the life stories of individuals who have overcome challenges and achieved success through a growth mindset.
- ✓ **Extract Lessons:** Identify common themes and lessons from these stories that you can apply to your own growth journey.
- ✓ **Share and Inspire:** Share these success stories with others to inspire them on their own paths of growth and development.

Final Thoughts and Reflections

As you conclude this comprehensive exploration of developing a growth mindset, take a moment to reflect on your personal insights and experiences. Recognize the progress you've made and the potential that lies ahead as you continue to embrace a growth mindset.

Action Plans and Strategies:
- ✓ **Gratitude:** Express gratitude for the opportunities you've had to learn, grow, and evolve.
- ✓ **Self-Compassion:** Practice self-compassion and kindness as you reflect on your journey, acknowledging both successes and challenges.

✓ **Commitment:** Reaffirm your commitment to nurturing a growth mindset and making it an integral part of your daily life.

Remember, a growth mindset is a lifelong pursuit that empowers you to embrace challenges, learn from failures, and continuously evolve into the best version of yourself. By integrating the lessons, strategies, and insights from this journey, you embark on a path of endless possibilities and personal transformation.

Conclusion

As you reach the conclusion of **'The Growth Mindset Blueprint-** *Transforming Challenges into Triumphs'* take a moment to reflect on the incredible journey of transformation you've undertaken. You've explored the depths of your mindset, challenged your beliefs, and embarked on a path of self-discovery that has the power to shape your life in profound ways. The insights, strategies, and exercises you've encountered are not just concepts to ponder, but tools to wield as you navigate the ever-changing landscape of your aspirations.

Your understanding of a growth mindset has evolved from a concept to a way of life. You've learned that challenges are not roadblocks, but stepping stones on your journey to success. Failures are not signs of defeat, but valuable lessons that propel you forward. Every effort you invest, every setback you encounter, and every step you take is a testament to your commitment to growth.

By embracing the power of a growth mindset, you've set yourself on a trajectory of continuous improvement. Your resilience in the face of adversity, your willingness to learn and adapt, and your capacity to cultivate positivity in every circumstance have become the cornerstones of your personal and professional endeavors.

Remember, the journey doesn't end here. Your growth mindset is a living, breathing entity that thrives on practice, consistency, and self-awareness. It's not about achieving perfection; it's about embracing the imperfections as opportunities to refine and redefine yourself. Keep the flame of curiosity alive, seek challenges that stretch your limits, and let every experience be a canvas for your growth.

As you move forward, continue to revisit the pages of this book. Reengage with the exercises, reflect on the stories, and reinforce the principles that have become the pillars of your growth journey. Your potential knows no bounds, and with each step you take, you inch closer to the remarkable person you are destined to become.

Thank you for joining me on this enlightening expedition of self-discovery and transformation. May your days be filled with a growth mindset that propels you to new heights, empowers you to overcome any obstacle, and guides you toward a future brimming with achievements and fulfillment.

Here's to the boundless possibilities that a growth mindset unlocks and to the incredible journey that lies ahead.

About the Author
'GERARD ASSEY'

Gerard Assey is a Graduate in Economics, a PGD in Management (HRD) and holds a Doctorate in Leadership. Gerard holds several International Qualifications in Sales, Debt Collection, Training & Teaching, and is a 'Fellow' of the prestigious 'Institute of Sales & Marketing Management'-UK, a Certified NLP Practitioner, a 'Certified Trainer', an 'Accredited Management Teacher-Behavioral Sciences', a 'Certified Competency Facilitator', a 'Certified Management Consultant'- (the International credentials of a professional management consultant, awarded in accordance with global standards of the ICMCI); and a Certification from the University of Michigan in 'Successful Negotiation: Essential Strategies and Skills'

He is also a Member of the 'National Association of Sales Professionals' backed with several years experience in varied industries, both in India and Overseas. He also holds an 'Etiquette Consultant' Certification from the USA (by Sue Fox, Author of Best Seller: 'Business Etiquette for Dummies'. She has trained some of the top celebrities' world over). He was also a recipient of a scholarship for extensive training in Japan on 'Corporate Management for India'.

Gerard Assey is 'Founder & Chief Corporate Trainer' of the Group: **'Citius, Altius, Fortius Unlimited'**- an organization that **celebrated 20 years of Glorious Service** in 2021, focusing on 3 Core Competencies:

People. Performance. Profit; in functional areas of Sales & Marketing, HR & Organizational Development, covering Recruitment, Training & Consultancy!

Having managed organizations with large Sales Forces in India & Overseas, his specialization cover extensive areas of Sales Training (All levels - Presentation, Negotiation, Key/ Strategic Accounts Management & Managerial Skills for all sectors), Bid Proposal/ Capture Planning/ Management Trainings, Retail Sales, Customer Service & Customer Retention Programs, Training for Prevention & Collection of Debt, Self & Personal Development Programs (Time Management, Teamwork & Team Building, Business Etiquette & Personal Grooming, Leadership & Managerial Skills, People Management Skills, Train-the-Trainer etc), including preparation of Custom-designed Business Manuals for Internal (HR, Induction, and Sales etc) & External use (Instruction, User Manuals).

Gerard has successfully conducted over 6080 Trainings & Workshops (as of Feb '24) all across India, Middle East, Africa, Europe & S.E. Asia. Besides public programs conducted regularly, both in India & Overseas, he has some of the top names as clients whom he services from Single Owners to large Public & Government undertakings, covering all sectors, for their in-house needs.

His website: www.CollectionSkills.com is the only one in this part of the world to be featured in the 'Collections & Credit Risk Magazine-USA' under 'Who's Who in Training' and ranks TOP, along with other websites listed below on most search engines.

Gerard is author of 114 books already (Mar 2024)

A few of our business related books:
1. Bite-sized Bits on Commonsense Management
2. Heart to Heart on Life's Principles'
3. How to become a Successful Manager
4. The Sales Professionals' Master Workbook of S.Y.S.T.E.M.S
5. The Professional Business Email Etiquette Handbook & Guide
6. The Professional Business Video-Conferencing Etiquette Handbook & Guide
7. Professional Presentation Skills
8. Exceptional Customer Service
9. Professional Tele-Marketing Skills
10. Professional Debt Collection Skills
11. The G.R.E.A.T. Sales & Service Workbook
12. Sales Training Advantage for Results (*The Ultimate Sales Training Manual to enable you stand out as a S.T.A.R.*)
13. CEO Daily Planner & Organizer
14. The Sales Professionals' Master Daily Planner
15. The Professional Debt Collector's Master Daily Planner
16. My Daily Planner & Organizer
17. MY EMERGENCY INFORMATION RECORD (Family Emergency & Peace of Mind Planner)
18. The Ultimate Therapist & Counselors Planner and Organizer
19. Building an Ethical Workplace
20. Managing Relationships at Work
21. Managing Business Meetings Effectively
22. Effective Delegation Skills
23. Goal Setting for Success
24. B2B Selling by Email
25. Professional Business Etiquette & Grooming
26. Dining Etiquette & Table Manners
27. Effective Networking Skills
28. Grooming, Etiquette & Manners for Teens, Young Adults & Future Leaders
29. Inter-Personal Skills
30. Get Ready, Get Hired!
31. Selling in a Recession
32. Effective Receivables Management in an Economic Downturn!
33. Real Estate & Property Sales Training

34. Credit Sales & Accounts Receivable Management
35. Selling Skills for Real Estate & Property Advisors
36. Take G.R.E.A.T. C.A.R.E!
37. Spa, Salon & Health Club Selling Skills
38. Selling Travel, Holiday & MICE Services
39. Selling Skills for Spa's, Salons & Health Clubs
40. Retailing in Salons & Spas
41. Selling Holiday, Vacation, Tours & Packages
42. The Power of Sales Referrals
43. Selling Luxury
44. Technical Selling Skills
45. Financial Advisors Sales Training
46. Dealing with Burnout at Work Monopolize Your Markets
47. Selling to Affluent Customers
48. Growing up with Grace
49. Financial Selling Skills
50. *The Effective Manager's Guide: Key Skills to Thrive*
51. From Aspiring to Inspiring: A Guide for New Managers on the Rise
52. The Power of Focus
53. Selling with Integrity: Sell Like Jesus The Perfect Role Model!
54. 31 Habits of Champions: Your 31-Day Journey to Greatness
55. Rejecting Grasshopper Talk: From Grasshopper to Giant-Killer-*Defeating Giants Daily!*
56. Navigate the AI-Powered Future of Bid & Proposals: Up-Skill to Stay Relevant with Alternative Career Paths & Opportunities
57. Hiring Sales Winners
58. Present with Impact
59. Success Unlocked: *Breaking Free from Habits that Hold You Back*
60. Complaints to Cheers, Feedback to Gold: Mastering Complaints Management
61. Thriving Together: *Cultivating Diversity, Equity, and Inclusion*
62. Coaching Skills for Sales Managers
63. Soaring to Success in Business & Leadership: Swifter, Higher, Stronger!
64. From Classroom to Podium: A Student's Guide to Powerful Public Speaking & Presentation Skills

65. Developing Self-Discipline
66. The CEO's 31-Day Power Plan: Unlocking Success through Essential Traits
67. Credibility Matters
68. A Winning Attitude
69. Bid & Proposal Management Using AI
70. Sales Forecasting: A Practical & Proven Guide to Strategic Sales Forecasting
71. Elevate & Energize: *50 Dynamic & Fun Activities for Peak Workplace Morale*
72. 'Sales SOS! Sales on Fire! *30 Days to Conquer Chaos & the Nightmares of Success!*'
73. Mastering Sales Managerial Skills: *Building High-Performing Teams & Driving Exceptional Results*
74. Eagle-Eyed Leadership: Unleashing the Power of 31 Lessons from Eagles
75. The Ultimate Employee Training Guide: *Training Today, Leading Tomorrow*
76. Being More Accountable at Work
77. Creating a Culture of Continuous Improvement
78. Effective Questioning & Listening Skills
79. The Power of Value Selling
80. The Growth Mindset Blueprint

Besides regularly contributing to business & trade journals, including international ones such as the 'Creative Training Techniques' and the 'Sales News' of the U.S.A, He is also a member of several prestigious bodies & trade associations, having participated in many Conferences & Workshops in India & Overseas.

Prior to his last assignment of leading & managing a large MNC as head, Gerard had a 3-year stint in the Middle East as a Consultant with a leading British Consultancy Firm.

As the past 'Official Country Representative' for the International Business Award- 'THE STEVIES'-(the business world's own Oscar) for about 4 years- he ensured a few Indian companies that qualify for the same every year!

Gerard can be contacted at:
Email: training@Sales-Training.in,training@CollectionSkills.com
Websites:

     www.Sales-Training.in
     www.EtiquetteWorks.in
     www.CollectionSkills.com
     www.RetailSalesTraining.in
     www.SalesTrainingIndia.com
     www.ManualPreparation.com
     www.TrainingWithPuppets.com
     www.FirstContactAcademy.com
     www.SalesAndMarketingRecruiter.com

Our **TRAININGS** that can help your team

- ✓ **Sales Effectiveness**: Selling Skills for any Sector: Service/ Logistics/ FMCG Realty/ Insurance & Finance/ Media/ SPA's, Health Clubs & Salons/ Key Account Management, Effective Negotiation Skills/ Bid & Proposal Management Skills/ Retail Sales Training: Any Sector (Auto, Jewelry, Clothing, Luxury etc)
- ✓ **Customer Service Skills**-Complaints Handling & Customer Retention
- ✓ **Debt Prevention & Collection Skills**
- ✓ **Etiquette & Grooming**
- ✓ **Leadership & Managerial Skills**
- ✓ **Self & Personal Development Skills**: Presentation Skills/ Effective Communication Skills/Business Proposal Writing Skills/ Problem Solving & Decision Making Skills/ Empowering Secretaries-The perfect PA! (For Secretaries & PA's)/ Effective Time Management/ Teamwork & Teambuilding/ P.R.I.D.E- **P**ersonal **R**esponsibility **I**n **D**elivering **E**xcellence